Solitary Architectures

Solitary Architectures
Selected Poems

Kornelijus Platelis

Translated from the Lithuanian
by
Jonas Zdanys

LAMAR UNIVERSITY press

ISBN: 978-0-9915321-4-8
Library of Congress Control Number: 2014954847
Front Cover Painting by Willem Koekkoek

Manufactured in the United States of America

Lamar University Press
Beaumont, Texas

For all those who taught me the poetry
of two languages

Books from Lamar University Press

Jean Andrews, *High Tides, Low Tides: the Story of Leroy Colombo*
Charles Behlem, *Failing Heaven*
Alan Berecka, *With Our Baggage*
David Bowles, *Flower, Song, Dance: Aztec and Mayan Poetry*
Jerry Bradley, *Crownfeathers and Effigies*
Julie Chappell and Marilyn Robitaille, editors, *Writing Texas, 2013-14*
Robert Murray Davis, *Levels of Incompetence: An Academic Life*
William Virgil Davis, *The Bones Poems*
Jeffrey Delotto, *Voices Writ in Sand*
Gerald Duff, *Memphis Mojo*
Ted L. Estess, *Fishing Spirit Lake*
Mimi Ferebee, *Wildfires and Atmospheric Memories*
Ken Hada, *Margaritas and Redfish*
Michelle Hartman, *Disenchanted and Disgruntled*
Katherine Hoerth, *Goddess Wears Cowboy Boots*
Lynn Hoggard, *Motherland, Stories and Poems from Louisiana*
Dominique Inge, *A Garden on the Brazos*
Gretchen Johnson, *The Joy of Deception*
Gretchen Johnson, *A Trip Through Downer, Minnesota*
Christopher Linforth, *When You Find Us We Will Be Gone*
Tom Mack and Andrew Geyer, editors, *A Shared Voice*
Dave Oliphant, *The Pilgrimage, Selected Poems: 1962-2012*
Janet McCann, *The Crone at the Casino*
Erin Murphy, *Ancilla*
Harold Raley, *Louisiana Rogue*
Carol Coffee Reposa, *Underground Musicians*
Carol Smallwood, *Water, Earth, Air, Fire, and Picket Fences*
Jim Sanderson, *Trashy Behavior*
Jan Seale, *Appearances*
Jan Seale, *The Parkinson Poems*
Melvin Sterne, *The Number You Have Reached*
Robert Wexelblatt, *The Artist Wears Rough Clothing*

For more information about these and other books, go to
www.LamarUniversityPress.Org

Acknowledgments

This book is published in cooperation with The International Cultural Program Center program "Books from Lithuania." I am most grateful for that generous support. I am also grateful to Sacred Heart University for granting me faculty release time to work on this collection and on other volumes.

Some of the translations in this collection as well as revised introductory remarks have appeared in *Vėjo namai/A Home for the Wind: An Anthology of Lithuanian Haiku* (2009), *Snare for the Wind* (1999), and *Four Poets of Lithuania* (1995).

CONTENTS

xiii   Introduction

From *Words and Days* (1980)
17   Milk and Tomatoes

From *A Home on the Bridge* (1984)
18   Overtaken Fog
19   An Encounter at Dusk
20   A Poem About Solitary Architecture
21   My Grandmother's History

From *A Snare for the Wind* (1987)
23   Proteus
24   Midday
25   Breaking Glass
26   Secret Conversations
27   The Descending Swan
28   Starlings
29   Czech Etude
31   Ghosts
33   An Empty House
34   Morning Concert

From *The Boat Shell* (1990)
36   Zone
37   Nihilists
38   On the Other Side of the Glass
40   Raise High the Mast, Carpenters!
41   Bookish Vengeance

From *Orations to the River* (1995)
43   Apocrypha
44   The Jinn
47   The Glance
48   The Raven
49   The Start of Hunting Season
50   Restorers

From *Tidal Zone* (2000)

52 Fisherman
53 I Don't Worry About Culture
54 Rodeo
55 Tidal Zone
56 The Top
57 Night's Melancholy
58 About Starlings Ten Years Later
59 Apples
60 Hades Kidnaps Persephone
61 St. Elizabeth's Hospital

From *Palimpsests* (2004)

63 The Tiller of the Soil
64 Waking in Silence
65 An Ordinary Meeting
66 Primavera
67 Time to Write and Time to Change
68 The Woman in Front of the Shop Window
69 An Ordinary Ascent
70 Campo de Fiori
71 The Magi
72 Passover
74 Nobody
76 Another Rendezvous
78 Birdie
79 Palimpsests
80 A Cry in Sleep
81 Spring in the Middle of Fall

From *Cave Phenomena* (2010)

82 A Shabby Dwelling
84 A Discussion About Lions
85 The Goddess of Oblivion
86 Outlines
89 About Starlings After Yet Another Five Years
90 Portrait
91 The Faceless
92 Autumn's Flowers
93 The Square

94   Vita Nuova

95   A Troubled Year

96   Also Died

97   Wanting to Be

99   I Met that Starling Later in Dublin

100 Confrontation in the Museum

101 Cave Phenomena

103 The Transfigured Stairs

New Poems

104 Haiku, Senryu, and Other Very Short Poems

110 The Carp

111 The Ebony Tower

112 Fragmentation: Phrygians

113 The Difficulties of Integrating into Society

114 Notes

115 About the Translator

Introduction

Kornelijus Platelis was born in 1951 in Šiauliai, in northcentral Lithuania. He graduated from the Vilnius Building Institute in 1973 and worked until 1988 as an engineer in Druskininkai, a resort town in southern Lithuania along the banks of the Nemunas River. He published his first poems in 1977 and is the author of eight collections of verse: *Žodžiai ir dienos* (Words and Days, 1980), *Namai ant tilto* (A Home on the Bridge, 1984), *Pinklės vėjui* (A Snare for the Wind, 1987), *Luoto kevalas* (The Boat Shell, 1990), *Prakalbos upei* (Orations to the River, a volume of selected poems, 1995), *Atoslūgio juosta* (Tidal Zone, 2000), *Palimpsestai* (Palimpsests, 2004), and *Karstiniai reiškiniai* (Cave Phenomena, 2010). His extended essay on the ecology of culture, *Būstas prie Nemuno* (Being by the Nemunas), was published in 1989, and his collection of essays on poetry, *Ir mes praeiname* (And We Are Passing), appeared in 2011. He has also translated many of the most important American, British and Irish poets—among them John Keats, Ezra Pound, T.S. Eliot, e.e.cummings, Ted Hughes, and Seamus Heaney —and Polish poets Adam Mickiewicz, Czesław Miłosz, Adam Tadeusz Naruszewicz, and Wisława Szymborska. He was also instrumental in developing commentary for a new Lithuanian edition of the Bible. His work has been translated into Armenian, Belarusian, Chinese, Czech, English, Estonian, French, Gaelic, Galician, Georgian, German, Hungarian, Italian, Japanese, Korean, Latvian, Macedonian, Norwegian, Polish, Russian, Slovenian, Spanish, Swedish, and Ukrainian, and has appeared in various anthologies and editions.

In 1988 Platelis joined the democratic liberation movement Sąjudis, and after Lithuania reestablished its independence from the Soviet Union he served in the administration of Vytautas Landsbergis as Vice Minister for Culture and Education and as Minister of Education and Science in the administration of President Valdas Adamkus. He has also served as Deputy Mayor of Druskininkai, as Director of the VAGA

Publishing House, and from 2001 until 2014 as Editor-in-Chief of *Literatūra ir menas* (Literature and Art), the leading Lithuanian literary and cultural journal. He serves currently as President of the Lithuanian Association of Creative Artists, as a Member of the Board of National Radio and Television, as Vice Chairman of the Fund for Press, Radio and Television, and as Chairman of the Board of the international annual literary festival "Druskininkai Poetic Fall." Among his many honors and awards is the Lithuanian National Award for Culture and Arts (2002) and fellowships and grants from Lithuanian and Scandinavian sources.

Platelis' poetry, as the work in this selection illustrates, is a mixture of political and declarative styles on the one hand and mystical intensity, metaphysical questioning, and exploration of myth on the other. At its core is active affiliation with the sensibilities of a generation of writers who, as Platelis describes them in his essay "On the Civic Role of Poetry," were nihilists when they began their creative work, women and men with a violated system of values whose work is futuristic or hermetic and whose aesthetic sensibilities are motivated by a certain artistic and cultural rebellion that is itself the product of a "contradictory reality." The work of the poets of his generation, Platelis believes, constitutes the frame of the renaissance of contemporary Lithuanian poetry. Their poems are concerned with the ultimate search for beauty and with the hope of the possibility of realizing that goal, and they approach that search through poetic experimentation marked by aestheticism and light decadence, where artifice and complexity are guiding and foundational creative propositions.

Platelis' poetry, though, aims at a higher plane as well, one on which questions of personal and social ethics and the possibility of an ethical culture can be considered and resolved. In that effort, Platelis is concerned with the revivification of individual and cultural biography, in which there is a need to recognize and atone for the "faults / we gathered in the labyrinth of history." The process of that atonement, for Platelis, finds its most powerful resonance in the heroic dimensions of the human spirit—often presented through the guideposts of myth—and in their linkages to absolute moral values, which are tied as well to aesthetic and cultural principles. It is a theme he explores in *Būstas prie Nemuno*; it is a theme that resonates with certainty in much of his poetry; and it is motivation that has led him to the liberation movement and government service in two areas—education and culture—which he believes are essential to national amelioration as well as personal redemption.

Because of his broad cultural engagements and interests, or perhaps because his aesthetic and personal predilections have propelled him to such engagements beyond the realm of poetic intersections with the world, Platelis encourages all of us—as a human collective and as a gathering of responsible individuals—to accept an active role in forging an ethical sense of self within an enlightened moral and cultural context.

These elements reflect a distinctive postmodernist strain in his work. Like a handful of other postmodernists on the contemporary poetic stage in Lithuania, Platelis also hides behind masks of his own creation, not because he does not believe in the ethical values he professes but because he does not believe in the act of such profession or in the ultimate validity of the professor. Such proclamations, after all, are human in their dimension, and in his poems Platelis knows that his imaginings are conditional, that his ability to render a complicated and multilayered reality in absolute terms is imperfect.

Platelis' poetry is important for other reasons as well, not the least of which are his sense of the overwhelming power of history and his understanding and exposition of its Orwellian dimensions. What saves us all, he says, in the dark light of such madness, is the possibility that we can indeed discover counterpoints to spiritual terror. Those counterpoints, which can shape individual lives and the nation's existence for the good, can be found in the affirmation of the role played by love and by the imagination in combatting the legacy of fear and alienation that has defined the postwar Lithuanian experience and, in fact, which has foundationally shaped human civilization.

In Platelis' poetry, the powers of love and of imagination often work in concert and in the face of difficult odds to sustain the human heart and spirit. The result is transcendence and Platelis provides lucid touchstones on that journey. By encouraging, in his own persuasive way, opportunities for personal as well as social liberation and freedom, and the individual as well as collective ethical realignment such opportunities make possible, Platelis has rightfully earned a prominent place among the writers of his generation.

I have selected for inclusion in this volume poems from all of Platelis' published collections as well as poems that have not yet been gathered together in a book. I was guided in that process by suggestions and conversations with Platelis himself, through letters and emails and in person during my visits to his home and his visits to mine. I am most grateful for his cooperation and encouragement during the course of my work on this book. I could not have asked for a more gracious or engaged partner in the process of rendering these poems in ways in which I believed they spoke and sang most clearly.

J.Z.

Milk and Tomatoes

she left a note: dearest
buy two bottles of milk and two
tomatoes he thought for a long time
having read the note sitting on the kitchen
stool how white milk is in a glass
creamy and white
as the skin of her face
it will flow past lips into the belly
then she will wipe herself with a white
napkin while tomatoes
are red as lips their juice
flows down the marble chin
until a white hand wipes it away
(tomatoes are so juicy!)
her eyes will shine with desire
she will be wearing a white dress
or a checked skirt

he will definitely buy
two bottles of milk and two
tomatoes

Overtaken Fog

Her golden hair
Flames like the first sacrifice of harvest in the green fields
And her feet glitter.

Overtake her. (The moment of union intoxicating—
It is the inconceivable realization of form,
The lightning-quick "yes" and the thunder
Immediately echoing away.)
Overtake her with words?

Her feet root suddenly in the soft ground.
Her hands turn to branches.
Her gentle waist is covered by coarse bark (the present
Grows strangely between her ribs)—a laurel tree.

And the days grow brighter,
Joy penetrates the joints
Like evening fog on the river.

An Encounter at Dusk

While looking out the library window
At the dusk of winter,
The shelves suddenly open and a boy enters
Carrying a basket of apples and roses.
And the darkness thickens, thoughts tangle.
Today—he says—
A very strange thing happened to me:
I was walking down the orchard path and found myself
In a gloomy room with shelves
Filled with rectangular slabs.
A sad man stood there looking out the window
At the dusk of winter.

A Poem About Solitary Architecture

Stiff towers in the long autumn rain
Pierce the stony sky.
Pigeons and crows find shelter there
From the city's noise.
Half-savage cats
Read the letters of rooftops and walls, swallows
Understand the conversations of ledges.
A cold wind walks the archways,
Fingers the pediments,
Measures the width of columns, ponders
The symbolism of plans and facades.
And throws into my eyes
The fine dust of disintegration—the only common language
That I know
And is known by the long loneliness of these buildings.

My Grandmother's History

In the corner, aloe.
She had round-rimmed glasses.
A cat mewled beneath her window
And dust settled on her gramophone.
Talking about the past she would say: *consummatum est*
Or something else in Latin.
She especially loved one philosopher. Caligula, I think.
But we were so involved in this world....

When she died
I inherited everything.
Most important, the gramophone on which I would play
Popular songs until I went mad,
And the cat beneath the window, in which in the evening
Sunsets glowed, and for the first time
I experienced how old the world is.
Even before proclaiming myself divine.
And later my gramophonic mouth matured,
My thoughts cleared, and my whole body
Mewled sadly whenever its surface
Was touched by the fingers of aloe-tinged memories,
And divine dreams danced in the dust of madness—
Such sweetness!

Perhaps the world is older than my grandmother—
I said scattered among its shapes—
If the soul melted without overcoming resistance
And gives itself victories only at night
In erotic twilights. And in the end
I understood how hard the road is
That led from my grandmother's house,
What angry god gave us our hopes and days.

And songs played on the gramophone also grew old,
Went out of style, and the cells of my body,
Having turned to dust, so dulled the needle

That in the evenings I began to drink boiled milk
And trembling with pleasure
Watched my neighbors' lives.

The hours are so deep, and if
My grandmother had sunken into them without pain
She would have much to be grateful for
To the healing properties of aloe.

Proteus

Consciousness loses its way among the words of lies
In day's delusions and night's metaphors.
At the crossroads
I set a trap for the beast.
At night the weathervane creaked,
Someone grieving in an owl's voice
Tossed about in the spider webs of my contemplations.

What can I say to the man who strangles me?
What face do I reveal? Masks like wet snow
Fall and melt on his dirty hands,
On the paws of everyday,
That reek of bodies, food,
The sweat of nerves.

Tracks of a strange beast,
Ropes burst apart,
Morning dew on paper—
My face?

Midday

A light wind ripples through the wild poppy
Blossoms, brushes across my face
With the fragrance of drying straw, reminding me
Of love's promises in the shade of blooming lindens.
The clouds are like tangled bodies
On pale blue sheets.
I asked suddenly:
Midday, where is your essence?
And it answered me: in this grass among blossoming
Wild poppies, in the skull of a sitting man,
In that skull are many gray cells, in those
Cells many words, among those words—one
Which is my essence, but no one
Knows it: not that man nor I.

Breaking Glass

When I see you walking by
Easy and short-lived
As a morning in May
And I want to call you, touch you, stop you,
Those who live with me,
Standing just over my shoulder, sigh heavily
With cold breath on my neck.

And my head drops,
My voice freezes in my mouth,
The smile fades from my lips.

Only my hand, as if on its own, stutters toward you
Brushing against the bottles,
And the sound of breaking glass fills the room.

You disappear beyond the misty edge of consciousness
Frightened by the noise,
Muse of the poetry of love.

Secret Conversations

You talk and talk, having forgotten
That you are talking with the dead.
Their words shape their faces,
Their thoughts quicken your blood,
And someone begins to talk to you
As if talking to the dead.

Horizons of the living murmur
With the monotone drone of the sea.

The Descending Swan

Into the pond's mirror
A swan descends silently
And its reflection
Perches on the bottom of evening
And its black feet
Touch the top of the water
And both swans melt into one.

Bending down you whisper something to me without a sound
Then put your head on my shoulder
And disappear behind the fluttering shroud of dreams.

Starlings

My son asked me to build a bird house
For a starling and we worked hard together
All afternoon to build it properly from the start
And cut and planed and shaped the boards.
And so the house outside the window here.
The starling is expecting children, whistles
Every morning on the birdhouse pole, while
I sit at my desk and write down something new
Believing that the two of us are kin
And that our distinct but dedicated trills and songs
Spread out through different communities
Though the meaning of our songs is probably the same.

Czech Etude

Tobacco smoke
Billows among the tables like a river
Across the stones of heads. On a small round table
A glass of beer and cooked liver sausage.
A pale woman quietly approaches
And tugs on my sleeve.
My eyes are locked on the haunches of a waitress,
My mouth full of fatty cud, my fingers convulsively
Fondle the glass' handle, but she approaches
Once again and says: it's time
And we go out into the wet autumnal street.

Each journey is like a death
And poetry—says the young man dressed in black
In the violet rain by the door.
You leave the cozy tavern,
Your comfortable circle of drinking friends, only to
Wake up in a cold room among scattered masks,
Torn formal wear,
Things ravaged by the whirlwind of passion,
Alongside the woman who sleeps enigmatically,
The white oval of her face turned to the moon.
Before dawn the man gets up, lights a cigarette,
Walks across the cell, persistently looking for the door.
As the sun rises this room
Begins to look like an office
Which could best be described by the gloomy and pedantic
Jew from Prague, Joseph K.,
And in the evening, once again a tavern
Where thick-hipped
Romantic poetesses force you to feel
Love for the world of things.
But woman is only one—
Says the young man, wiping his lips
With a fragrant handkerchief.
The one who wakes in late afternoon, stretches, gets up,

Goes out of the rib cage with predacious steps.
One like a journey
From birth to death.

Ghosts

Therefore when Tao is lost, there is Te.
When Te is lost, there is kindness.
When kindness is lost, there is justice.
When justice is lost, there is ritual.
Now ritual is the husk of faith and loyalty,
the beginning of confusion.
            Lao Tse. *Tao Te Ching,* 38

Paris.
The train comes to a slow stop, blows steam,
The conductor gives the signal, rational
Jurists shout "hoorah"—Kung Tse climbs down the stairs
Smiling mysteriously. Then the orchestra
Lets fly in such a way that the visitor squats frightened
And scatters his principles of harmony.
It's the end of the 18th century—sentimental
Burghers, clean rivers, fields fertilized with manure...

But then the emperor
Ch'in Shih Huang Ti decides for all time
From the heights of Mo Tse's teachings
To criticize Confucius' supporters, that's why they
Are buried alive in the ground and quickly suffocate
Under the happy Empire's body—
The correction of names, the correction of lives
According to the matrices of death... Although words
Quickly swell with blood and become as sluggish
As satiated ticks.

And only the accomplices of the buried
Quickly cut the ropes and head for the mountains,
On every road on the look out for the emperor's armed horsemen.
Donkeys carry rolls of books.
And later from Tibet we receive a note
In which the escapees, having rummaged through their brains,
Demand orators
Who explain the ritual, from aesthetic and ethical perspectives,

Punish them with physical punishment—
Twenty strokes of bamboo sticks on each sole.

The dragon is reborn from its own
Ashes. At first so beautiful and kind,
So pure and attractive,
Swinging in the bodies of sages, having secured itself
Between the word and consciousness.
And works its way through all barriers
Like the virus of typhoid fever.
And then it is too late—bile floods
Our desolate hearts and famished teachings
Incarnate themselves in real time: at night
Black echelons begin to move from darkened stations
To nowhere, unloading the dead
Along the way like mail. And our
(Association of Ghosts) chancellery
Doesn't manage to stamp the personal
Papers of all the spirits...

And all that is missing is one basketful
To complete the mountain
And the world rolls forward
Along its only road
And the dead are not connected to these things,
Completely not connected.

An Empty House

The floor creaks sharply
As I walk through the house,
The door groans, the cuckoo,
Popping out of the rusted clock,
Sings three times into the deaf afternoon
And a pale boy
Casts an angry glance at me
From around the corner.

That's how we meet in our indivisible land—
A man from the marketplace and a lost giant—
Beneath a sun setting into dust.
A rock like a bolt of lightning
Cuts the thick air, and slain I fall
Face down into my ancestors' cold ashes.

An empty house. On the window sill
A vase with the hyacinth
Of my pagan soul. The spring wind
Suddenly blows in through the broken window
And stirs the ashes in the hearth.

Morning Concert

The sun cascades into the littered room
Through dirty curtains.
A table splashed with beer where several naiads
Sleep draped
Among scraps of food. A young man
Blows on a jabbering flute. She brings over
A tub of water, puts it on the dirt floor and slowly
Begins to undress. The music teacher
Starts to play a monotonous song. She puts
Her left foot into the water, bends over and...
My body suddenly shivers, my face reddens,
Hot steam through the nostrils bristles the hair of those still sleeping,
The hardening forehead aches, fists turn into hooves,
A holy picture falls from the wall caught by a horn
And breaks into a thousand mirror splinters.
What did I see, God, what did I see?
It's a miraculous sign involuntarily and unintentionally
Opening the secrets of the world and heart,
The sources of truth and power!
Things brighten, there is a fragrance of incense.
The head is wrapped in the stiff ringing of space.

Dogs barked terrifyingly outside.
The teacher choked on a sound,
The young man threw away the flute.
I tried to speak but the two of them
Gaped at each other and squealed like pigs.
Deer—I thought—only deer in forest valleys
Could understand the meaning of lofty words.
Then, through the door out
Into the bright autumnal air. Hounds
Cling to the joints.
No one
Will know I am forced to leave my body
To the red jaws of dogs.
Together with the instruments of speech.

Together with the will to speak.
Blood spatters the grass.
A net of curtains.
A gate of forged iron.
Time slamming shut.

Zone

Where does it end, where does it begin?
Ventilation pipes on the flat roof drone
Like eternity. The landing force,
As they are called, climbs
On a metal truss that holds silos of sawdust,
To the chimney extending
From the varnishing shop, reach the top
And smell the terrifying mix of odors
That the ventilator vomits into the darkened sky,
Holding on to the metal beam
With arms and legs.
They hang that way until they shake off
This world and fall in
To the zone.

The physician's assistant, cursing,
Puts casts on arms and legs,
Wipes blistered lips
And noses with stinking ointment.
The landing force, as they are called,
One by one return in
To the zone.

Nihilists

One form of nihilism is Plato's
When he, as Heidegger affirms,
Sees Existence having forgotten Being.
Another nihilism is the young man's
For whom it is the same to spit at Being
And beings as he struts into a bar
Fingering the money in his pocket
And looks at all the girls, making plans for the night,
And sitting down at a table
Discourses to the red-nosed around him
About the vanity of the world.
Still another is the nihilism of the poet
Who understands nothing sufficiently
But who worries about saying ever more.

On the Other Side of the Glass

During the night frost
rewrote the landscape
in its own hand.

*

On fresh snow
only a black cat
with a white chest.

*

The forest has sunk into itself
while under thick ice
the river trickles silently.

*

"I"—like a mountain
in the river of perception
across the ice floes.

*

It snows on the waiting
orchard brides
in beggarly bits.

*

In the bowl of the silver
pond the moon
is like a round fish
between two lovers
who swallow it with their eyes

*

After a night rain
the garden fainted with joy,
dew in the calendula blossoms
shines with cathartic tears.

*

In the green ship
a deranged crew—the white
worm incites mutiny.

*

Across the night sky
a shrieking bird flew
from yesterday to tomorrow, from
the unknowable to the unknown.

*

And what sort of autumn is it without geese
making their way southwestward?
Yes, and here they are—
honk honk—barking away,
and we mark it down.

*

Leaves fall...
But first in the heart
the world passes away.

*

Pines with thin fingers
comb the fog.
Muffled church bells
fill their traces.

*

Wet tiles. Autumn.
Convolvulus
curls back into the ground.

*

A sad November morning—
the iron gates of my eyes
open as I wake.

Raise High the Mast, Carpenters!

Cracked boat shell—
Isn't it the one Gilgamesh used
To travel to that other shore,

To the land without time,
To the eternity of signs
Of a stiffened bolt of lightning?

Boards rot in the sand,
Speech and the soul die
In the valley of indecision.

The tree of language
Awaits the sap of our life,
The sails await our breathing.

Raise the mast, carpenters!
They return there as kings
With fruits made of diamonds.

Bookish Vengeance

They rode into our village
Creaking with rusted helmet visors
Led by a gray-bearded old man in whose eyes
Were endless faith, hunger and emptiness
And on whose chest was hammered
The sign of Saturn. They rode to avenge
Some offense against their god.
They killed a few boys and sick people
Who tried to resist. The men were gone.
They stopped beneath an oak tree
To catch their breaths. Then spread through the village.

The cries of women fill the cupola of heaven,
The impotent anger of old men
Penetrates stones,
Eats the eyes of the gods,
Crumbles the corners of the sky.
Terror and hopelessness flood
Through the cottage windows.
Beneath the sacred tree
Grows a mountain of infants.
Small bloody bodies
Shudder in the powdered snow.
Thin red streams flow to the middle of the street.

Someone tried to call out to god, but the earth opened
And swallowed him. Someone
Tried to speak but from his mouth
Came only the yelping of dogs.
They sat where they stood, held their heads
On hands of stone.
In the splinters of their world
As an unfamiliar wind blew through the cracks of the sky.
The morning star, lighting the road for the fugitives,
Found all the people of the village frozen
To tombstones of ice.

And the boys outside the village dug a long trench
Poking clumps of earth with spears.
Girls cooked food in their homes, concentrating on their work
As if fulfilling some ritual,
And the youngest children
Chased dogs away from the corpses with sticks
And sang something about the sun.

Apocrypha

On the road to Golgotha
Ahasuerus is still chasing the man with a cross
Away from his home while in Jerusalem's custom's-house
Scripture's decoders already compose secret documents,
Prepare visas for the apostles,
Study life in the diaspora, strengthen
The net of agents in Rome and in the provinces.
It is essential to evaluate correctly
The Grecian spirit, the hunger in their souls,
Their dreams, repeating for millennia.
(A man is nailed to a cross.)
The world is brutal and old. Ships of Gnosis
Abandon the exhausted civilization
And spread across the Mediterranean Sea, penetrate
Islands and seaside ports.
Reconnaissance multiplies the Apocrypha
About the human nature of god.
(Guards cast lots for his cloak.)
Wise men consider the game plan
And that, which is
Outside the game, remains for the condemned,
Remains for travelers on this earth, leaving
Meekly one by one, because theirs is the kingdom of death.
A few influential
Workers have plastic surgery.
The stone rejected by the builders
Is mentioned ever more often.
Candidacies of martyrs are considered.
In the beginning was Logos.

The Jinn

All those who distort truth and do harm
to the teachings of the Church are the
Samarian Simon Magus' apostles and disciples...
In truth—they do not carry before them the name
of Jesus Christ but in all manner teach us Simon's
godlessness ... pouring into the ears of the listener
the Great Serpent's (Satan's), the primal apostate's,
poison.

St. Iranaeus, *Adversus Haeresus*

You are mistaken, Samaelis, blind god.

Once we rode out on camels to Nag Hammadi—
I, Muhammad Ali al-Samman, and my brothers—
To bring fertilizing silt back to our fields.
While digging it we found a clay jug sealed tightly with a cork.
I was seized by fear. I thought
A jinn was in it.
But the hope to find gold lifted my pick.
Beneath the scattered fragments were thirteen papyrus
Books we brought home and piled near the hearth
In my life, mute, dreary, and stifling as the earth.
Perhaps only this metabolism is quicker: women
Sometimes used pages for kindling. That's how everything
Would have ended but a few weeks later Allah allowed
My brothers and me to sneak up on our father's murderer,
One Ahmed Ismail, and we then released
His despicable soul from his body, let it loose to the winds,
Chopped off his feet, hands, afterwards tore out his heart
And divided it with a knife and ate it raw the way we were taught
By the rites of vengeance, buried what remained under a juniper.
We were young and hot, were not afraid to kill and die.
The police began questioning us and we had to hide
Those books at a neighbor's. And they began to rise slowly
In the dim light of mind where they were burned in the spirit's flames,
Washed by the water of souls, this extract was carried by blood...
Whether we found gold or freed a jinn

I didn't know for a long time and, of course, felt sorry
About the gold, which I would have raked in for them,
But later I started to connect it all to my father's
And his murderer's deaths. Even though that spring
A great world war had ended, having spilled oceans of blood,
Having released winds of souls. Finding me, various
People asked how and when we had found those books.
In exchange, I asked what was written in them...
And eventually understood that the murderer of the tribe's stepfather,
Dying then on the cross, was the son of the Highest Deity.
Intoxicated by his death the Archons lost their vigilance
Because, it appears, death always worked to calm them—
The spring of danger disappears: the soul leaving the world
Carries light there where their understanding does not reach.
So through the open door wisdom flooded our hearts,
And the Archons' vassals had to labor hard
Until they tangled truth, distorted his words and origin,
Created clever writings and hierarchies supported by force,
So that in the hearths of existence books and people would quietly burn,
And there would be only one truth, which they called truth.
But I still don't know who, having filled the other jug
With blood, gave it to the thirsty spirits of the desert to guard,
Whose will he was fulfilling, and who suggested the way...
Who am I, after all, and whose hand governs me,
How much free will do I have, how much truth am I allowed to know?
I ask myself all the more often and all the more often forget to pray.

You are mistaken, Samaelis, god of the blind.

Explanation
I received a handwritten translation into English
Of this text from a Portuguese who called himself
A millionaire, though he made a living as a journalist
And looked a great deal like an antiques dealer.
I remember how, after the third gin and tonic in the littered

Bar in Seville, he began fumbling through his pockets (the TV
Was broadcasting a *corrida,* the one in which the famous matador
Died in the spring of 1992), until he finally found a soiled
And tightly folded piece of paper and gave it to me saying
That he had gotten the translation from an Arab friend of his
Who worked in some museum in Cairo.
But I have no doubt whatsoever that this is an Apocrypha
Even though real people and events are mentioned in it.
Muhammad Ali, a Moslem, reasons
Like a primer Gnostic who, after "A Thousand and One Nights,"
Had read some version of the "Apochryphon of John."
But I think this story is worthy of publication, so our
Reader would see by what sort of bloody sacrifices
The sweet-talking spirits of hell vomit
From their jaws those clever error-filled heresies. I added
The epigraph myself, because I think it especially fits
Publication of the text in Lithuania. Its first line
Is a quotation from one of the Nag Hammadi codex of books,
"The Essence of the Archons" and the last from "About the Origin of the
        World."
In both instances it is the response of the Absolute to him who said:
"I am god and there is no other god before me!"

The Glance

She pushes through dark dust-filled rooms
In a white wedding gown to a space washed in sunlight,
She explodes like a clear ball of fire
Along the line of dark buildings like years
Into a neat square framed by bindweed,
Glancing covetously for the last time
At a light-haired young man with St. George's spear
On a white restless steed
Which will soon gallop through the thin curtain of death
Into an eternal morning,
Into a life which will immediately
Begin (everyone waits
Stretched to witness) and so—
Her eyes widened like two large caverns,
The dust-filled square already sinks down in menace,
Spurs press the steed and it heaves through the forehead,
Striking a spark of pain
And disappears on the other side of memory's intricate ornament.

Stains of blood spatter the soul's white linens.

The Raven

Most often it caws in the middle of the night
When the world is sunk deeply into the swampy
Kingdom of darkness and no voice
Stumbles behind things. And it vibrates
The thick walls of being, but not in the way
That E.A. Poe heard but with the small trumpets
Of a miniature Jericho—the clothing tears
And when it's gone a quiet resident remains
Who, waking, finds the television on,
A carpet with cigarette burned holes, and having forgotten
To take off the wrinkled formal wear—
NEVERMORE.

The Start of Hunting Season

Snow covers the forest. In the thickets
Hangs the heavy breathing of runners in the drifts.
The drivers zealously shake the resonant
Winter air, together with the sound
Exhaling a light vapor of homebrew.
Soon shell shots rain out,
Crows caw at the forest's edge.
First blood
Paints the hands and hides,
The operation room's sheets,
The white funeral linens....

The campfire's blue smoke rises into a gray sky.
A mournful hunting meal: smoked meat,
Warmth under the tongue, conversations about matters.
A storm rises,
The hounds of wind drive in hordes of white flies
And hurl them into the trees.
They pack their things and return quickly to an ordinary
Life, where the wind of time
Drives the souls of hunters to the line of death
And the wind of space lays down
On them the heaviness of an ordered world.

Restorers

We found a dancing foot in the tall grass.
A marble girl must have lost it, running
At night through our forests.
Sunset reddened her white glittering calf,
Of the kind only a goddess could have. Our breasts
Instantly filled with the power to recreate all of her,
So we quickly began
To form her missing joints from bee's wax,
Clinging to her like a piglet to a sow.
We talked curses, drew secret tokens,
Until the desired image
Began to shine in our foggy retinas.
She was like a goddess—long hair the color of wheat,
A young body coming clear under her thin garment,
Her hips trembled barely visibly,
Tense with a congealed hot wild dance.
Someone said the Our Father, someone wept.
We saw a flame
Pulsating beneath her thin skin, her breast
Rising with her breathing, the cunning soft stirring of her lips.
Because suddenly terror and madness flooded our veins,
Hands reaching for her paying no heed to our wills.
We held one another while consciousness did not abandon us.
Then we sang songs of love, angrily
Raising our fists to the emptied heavens.
(The world went on without us, we were not the same.)
And after that we began
To beat each other and when we saw first blood
We grabbed our axes.
Only one victor was left alive.
Under a clear midday sun
And the cold shine of the goddess' smile. All
Red with blood. He threw down his ax and shyly
Embraced the girl's slender waist.
Wax
Suddenly melted from the endless heat of his heart.

Yellow streams flowed down his face, shoulders, stretched
Down his torso until it covered all of him
And as he watched he stiffened to bronze.

Fisherman

In the box of my skull thoughts wriggle like worms,
the surface of the lake is still
as the mirror of the soul.
The fisherman's clumsy fingers grope for the worm,
mount it on the hook, the fishing line stretches on the water.
Shoulders crouch beneath a mantle of ermine.
What fish, what fish will he catch now?
Long as a spindle? Flat as a full moon?
Full of life's life? Death's death?
A fishing line tangling eel?
A hierarchical carp?
IXTHYS? Or perhaps nothing?
Perhaps his worms are not attractive
to the fish in this lake? Perhaps its mirror-like surface
has frozen to ice, and ice turned to steel,
separating these two worlds with a crust of death?
And no savior will come. From where would he come?
And who would he be—man, fish, or perhaps
a bolt of lightning, perhaps a puff of the spring wind?
The float dips under water. Ah, yes,
it's a poem's roach fish, a box,
the swarming worms of words.

I Don't Worry About Culture

The wild grape ends its choking
growth over the unpruned plum
whose branches will be broken by ripening fruits,
two young oaks already smother the cherries
in the garden corner. Everything is grown by *natura*,
it spreads within me, sending its vines through
my body's openings, winding around my soul,
like potato sprouts in a dark cellar becoming
something else, distorting ordinary
instincts and physiological needs.
The cherries grow smaller, sour, fruits
and consequences turn bitter. Spoiled wine
quickly carries me to black oblivion.

Rodeo

I jump on the bull's back, the gates open,
and the two of us break out into the arena of stinking sand
which has drunk its share of sweat, nose foam and blood,
and begin our reckless dance. Two currents
intersect, two wills grapple furiously,
and the result of their struggle—only an interruption,
so contemptibly small in the presence of eternity.
                              Falling
down, I manage to see a prudent
old man billowing on a bull's back
to the west, down river, down wind, the way time flows,
space and fluids gush through the arteries of the living.

Tidal Zone

She withdraws following the governing moon
with the waters and ghosts, with her creatures,
leaving behind the dark brown heads of stones
to stick up out of the shallows, coarse,
silt-covered footbridges among them,
clear puddles with seashells
and amphora shards sowing their bottoms, with
small fish brisk as thoughts, crustaceans slow
as contemplation, husks of bodies and souls
that for a moment connect the eye with the sun's light.

No man's land, unstable, but of stable rhythm,
a heron jumping from stone to stone
investigates the bottom with its beak and eyes,
the reefs' teeth hold back the great waters.

After the moon I drag the cloak of consciousness
and after the sun I try
to close up an image in a form.

The Top

We decided it was time to chop down
the early plum tree, in the summer giving us
a large harvest that no one needed.
Half of it was overrun by a wild grapevine
and a few of its branches were already drying.
But in the fall it unexpectedly loaded
with buds and exploded into white blossoms
right in the face of our somber thoughts.
Mad juices in the old trunk's veins,
the top like a bride's headdress
in the autumn rain.

Night's Melancholy

The heart is restless, the fragrant spring air
full of noise. She walks
through the garden gate and turns down the path
across the meadow, dressed severely, the only place
uncovered that small spot where the neck flows into the back,
face powdered, lips distinctly colored, eyebrows
thinly plucked, walks in small steps
at the edges of yards, hides in the alder grove,
appears again near the silvered brook where it
pours itself into the pond. The same moonlight is in her eyes.
She husks herself from the straight-lined dress—her white skin
is even paler against the wall of shadows—
and wades into the water which, uneasily turning colors,
pulls away from the foreign and unfamiliar body,
from the rank smell of perfume and perspiration, she bends
and two small snakes wind downstream—the red
of her lips and the pale dust of her powder,
the etheric oils of her perfume, everything
to the very foam of her body, to the disquiet of her soul.

Moonlight's silver is in the eye of the watching deer,
the intoxicating animal smell in the hounds' noses....

I still remember her raised arm
against a background of blossoming cherries, the outline
of her fingers above an embroidered sleeve, a few petals
in her raven-colored hair,
waving farewell.

About Starlings Ten Years Later

Remember—I wrote about a starling
Whistling outside the window? And now
Every spring it repeats itself
Even though the birdhouse is caked with droppings.
I too have written a sufficient number of lines,
And besides, the community's ear has changed.
It began to seem to me that the bird,
Singing the same songs all these years,
Knows how to sing without annoying,
But the poet, setting out the same words
In ever different ways, bores
Even himself. Besides, I have a home,
Became a father long ago—
So what should I call out for,
To what should I surrender my heart?
Nature falls asleep in my veins, spring
Becomes ever more like winter.
Our songs are different—his soars away
But mine lags behind the meaning
That the Creator gives to his feathered ones.

Apples

In trolley number 5 on the last seat
Next to a dozing old man from Gerontion,
A bag of red apples on my lap. Not for Paris,
Not for Alexander, but for my children, my family.
Unwittingly the apples of my breasts pulsate with juices.
The young man near the door across from me on the step,
Fixing his gaze on the apples, the juices, the reward,
Gathers, it seems, something from the shadows of his soul.
Between his legs the root of life begins to grow,
The uncontrollable horn stiffens, and he reddens in shame.
The old man, seeing that, wakes and begins to chuckle.
The young man, flustered, gets off at the first stop.
The old man continues chuckling, my body grows numb,
His juices begin to rage. I try to get out
At the next stop but my forgotten bag
Falls off my lap and the red apples spill out.
Undelivered reward. The old man laughs
And begins picking up the apples. Not for Alexander,
Not for Paris, but for my children, my family. I get off.
Back past the old voices, past the faces of Achivi.
May the gods send him his soul's most beautiful woman.

Hades Kidnaps Persephone

A fly bangs against the glass searching for a warm crack,
A saw's teeth greedily cling to wood,
Hades seizes Persephone in his arms, panting
Heavily he lifts her fat bottom off the ground,
The black harnessed steeds wait
And dig the soil with their hooves, fat-thighed nymphs
Wring their hands, bang against the cool air, weep
Like saws. Carelessly flowing
Time congeals into forms, life into its signs,
Water into flakes of snow, experiences into allusions
With which poetry is strewn, describing the bright landscape
Of life, diffusing the scent of Hades.

St. Elizabeth's Hospital

Our dynasty came because of a great sensibility.
Ezra Pound, Canto 85

Across the Anacostia River, among the trees,
St. Elizabeth slices a round cake
with a long shining knife and politely serves it
to the students of the poetry t-group waiting in line.
Their arms are bound along their bodies to the elbow,
their eyes as round as a cake sun,
they stretch oddly as they eat: it is the destiny
of poetry to repair consciousnesses and worlds. Suddenly
a telephone rings, calling for St. Elizabeth,
she hands over the knife and asks me to continue slicing.
As the long blade travels from one hand to the other
the sun bounces off and flashes in their eyes
chopping up their roundness like the knife
the cake. The world splinters
into myriad fragments and for a moment
congeals before crumbling. I

> Our dynasty came
> > because of a great sensibility.
> After all the pavilions of our palaces
> > I now look through John Howard's window.
> In the shadow of leafless trees
> > into the new age across the river.
> Our minds were somewhere else
> > when the gates opened.
> Our dynasty rested upon a strict hierarchy
> > contemplating beauty.
> The walls dissolved years ago
> > as I listened to forbidden places.
> Our dynasty established order in poetry
> > and gushed through the edges of form.
> Inner voice? Each of us got many
> > inner voices. Which would you like to hear?
> Our dynasty was hospitalized

because of its great faith.
The new world injected us with tranquilizers
                and our consciousnesses turned to wood.
St. Elizabeth took us into her care
                and love dissolved our will.
The founders of the world of equal values
                took to healing us with our own poetry.
The inexhaustible milk in St. Elizabeth's pitcher
                undermined the hierarchies' foundations.

stick the blade into the cake, splintered
reality holds together, an odd hope that already shined
through the cracks seals over. The poetry
t-group students meekly lower their eyes.
The balsam of words oozes through the cell walls—
glue of things and consciousnesses with bandaged arms—
the metal taste in my mouth is changed by the sweetness of cake,
returning us to harmonies, opening up
memory's roads to nowhere.

The Tiller of the Soil

J.

The wind above those fields feels free.
She presses against the ground like a hen as it rages.
In the sky, larks and clouds, and heavenly bodies
higher still, but she is interested only in the field,

the yearly plowing, the black soil that accepts
the seed and returns the plants,
and beneath the black only clay and gravel
empty as the azure sky, untillable.

And the small cemetery outside the village, on a sandy hill.
Her most beautiful garden is there—flowers, lawns—
as she weeds she rises ever higher—almost
everyone here is familiar—relatives or neighbors.

Once, when burying a cousin, they dug a hole
alongside her mother's grave, splitting off an edge of her coffin,
and she jumped into the hole to look in through the crack
to see how her mother felt there half a century later.

She was the same as when they buried her, only
black as a mummy, awaiting the last judgment
when she could reclaim her body; death's kingdom
is black as the soil, silent as the sky or sand.

Waking in Silence

Suddenly—silence,
a gloomy November morning
a chainsaw slices it
near the boundaries of consciousness,
the soul's rooms muddled,
unmade beds, leftovers,
     (You heard the bell,
      the primrose in the silver
      silence? No, it just seemed so.)
empty bottles everywhere, Elpenor dead,
a hollow echo.
     There is nowhere to hurry to.

An Ordinary Meeting

I met her again tonight: straight chestnut
hair, white skin, a red dress
with an odd wooden frame from hips to ankles
hobbling her steps.
But nothing stopped her, she walked
through fences, hedges, walls, only once
turning her head she looked at me
indifferently and walked off through the yard, walked
straight through the den where a pighead
half lying against a clay wall
stared at a gnawed son of man in the trough
as if he stared at himself.

Wait—I shouted—tell me what's happening
in these darknesses? She did not answer,
did not turn her head toward me
again.

Primavera

Midwinter spring is its own season.
T. S. Eliot, "Little Gidding"

The early February sun shining
straight into the window woke
a dappled butterfly, the kind summers
are filled with. Its delicate wings
rustled the luminous curtains' snow
and it drank the sun with its feelers
in my room, where only a laurel bush
is eternally green in a plastic vase,
where only naked dreams slip out of the dark
and return again, having left only
a coal-like footprint on the paper's snow.
And where will you return: back to sleep,
having experienced the seductions of sun and life,
when real snowflakes spin outside the window,
or to the eternity, unfamiliar and strange,
that these words cautiously try to establish?

*   *   *

The next day it lay on its back again,
prosy, its legs entwined on its belly,
as if laid out by skilled providers
of ritual services. The sky was overcast,
colors faded.

66

Time to Write and Time to Change

It's time to write lines but also time to change the oil. I drove
more than 20,000 km with the same. My car,
patiently and faithfully serving me, can no longer wait.
In the oily workshop among disassembled engine
parts, scattered tools, time presses my temples,
he talks on the phone, his pencil is a wrench, his paper—
the oily can, my pencil's at home,
but if my faithful one falls apart, all of my allotted time
will burst into flame, bare breasted women on the walls,
it's time to write letters and time to change the customs
of mechanical style, my faithful one—
is only a pile of metal, but all parts fit together,
my faithful one is not a woman but a machine,
my women, it's sad to say, are not so faithful,
there would be work for a mechanic in my soul too.
Finally a black stream stretches into the pail,
he changes the filter, signs in fresh oil.
A new time begins.

The Woman in Front of the Shop Window

She looked over the entire shop window, a beautiful
woman, still young, with a naked belly button
(that was the style), skin banal as a peach
in a poem. Spangles glittered in the window,
with which she liked to entice her prey– they alone
managed to give her glances any life—
metal sparkles
like brandished swords parrying against one another.
Hair, framing a carefully tended face,
asked not to be mussed,
and the stretched backs of her pants looked new,
a luxurious gravesite or slaughterhouse, if you'd like, for millions
of those small tadpoles that invade her
with hope and faith, and suddenly
knock against a rubber wall, some sort
of deadly foam or something even more sophisticated
because their mission ends right here, in a common grave
(for if it was different it would be even sadder), I saw
her wandering down the corridors of a tangled labyrinth—
robber of an empty grave, overcoming
obstacles and strange monsters,
beautiful, safely imprisoned on a flickering screen.

An Ordinary Ascent

I washed my face with Castillian water
so His eye could look at me undisturbed
and began to climb the steep Parnassian hill.

I had no statue in my hands, no question on my lips.
I was met by ruins. Wind walked
free among the columns.
No secret rooms were visible.

My skin reddened, but beyond it
nothing disturbed the darkness.

An ordinary rising of dust,
dust-covered shoes.

Campo de Fiori

A Bruno
Il Secolo Da Lvi Divinato
Qvi Dove Il Rogo Arse

On an early September afternoon
I looked through the window at Campo de Fiori—
the heat of the market was burning out, flowers tired of smiling,
dark stains spread under the tender skins of fruits,
a warm wind carried thin plastic shreds
like ashes, in the middle of the square raised from the ground
stood a blackened bronze man in a long cloak
and hood. It was Giordano Bruno, in his eyes
congealed campfire flames darkened to copper,
having devoured him here precisely four centuries ago
in the name of true knowledge.

Which, as is demonstrated by the facts we observe,
is carried by memory to be reborn in the soul's matrix
and shyly shows itself to God's reflection in its own depths,
and comprehension gushes forth knocking down reason's walls
like a river of flame that flows in both directions.
And the movement stops, the soul clenches
like an impregnated womb, and ... *We thank the Lord*
that we are not so blind, we do not affirm or judge
so therefore know—the fire of our hearts is hotter
than all the flames of this world. Silent fields of flowers
ripple beneath our feet, pistils wait for pollen,
their awareness is small but fragrant and durable,
bees carry them and wind as if ashes. Dried out blackberries,
wilting market flowers, the enticing sighs of death
on the misleading roads of knowledge.

The Magi

Through deep snow, numb with cold, led by undiscovered stars
from container to container carrying in plastic bags
recyclable goods like wombs giving birth to things,
using everything that helps them tear themselves away
from the world, whatever is convertible
into moments of ecstasy. Bodies like overworked mules.
Where are they being driven by their anxiety?
Perhaps they know something more, each night watching the cold
sky above their heads, so they build no homes, do not get settled,
do not earn bread by the sweat of their brows?

Directly beneath the North
Star, in one container
at the edge of town, they found a dead child
in a plastic bag. They gave him no gifts
and did not bury him, not wanting
to have any dealings with the police, they were
people of other customs, from another land.
They let him continue suffering quietly for our sins,
unburied, unmourned, unable to rise.
To suffer right away, without words, miracles, sermons,
because everything is already said, everyone is taught,
only action remains. The face of young
Janus in the plastic bag.

Perhaps they know something more?
Perhaps they wait for something to happen?

Passover

My mother told me how, on the second day of Easter,
she once took me to school with her
because she had no one to leave me with, and I walked
lagging behind her looking carefully at everything. Our street

was almost empty, but when she turned around she saw
an Easter egg in each of my hands, the government forbade
dyeing them then, Stalin had not yet croaked,
as my father used to say. She was afraid: perhaps someone

had deliberately pressed them insidiously into my hands
and some anonymous complaint would shortly reach the Party,
or perhaps someone wanted to show the schoolmaster, through her son,
that Easter was still alive in the catacombs of hearts.

Or perhaps—I think—it was some masculine god, having
passed here at night who took the unsacrificed firstborns
from among those whose doorposts were not marked by blood,
so tired of killing and satiated, that instead of

scratching a knife across my throat (I was after all
a firstborn, though outside, beyond the door, and there
was no blood on my forehead or hands, only baptismal water)
had deigned to leave reflections of his own eggs in my hands.

And because it was a god, those reflections were tangible,
and because of that, the community who worshipped that god
could confidently use his annual passage
for reasons bordering on the political, led by him to war.

Of course, that is the classic ideology of terrorism
which is used throughout the world, not only in Egypt or Palestine,
to employ noble goals to justify the means.
I can't say now that those Easter eggs freed me

from slavery, because when I joined the Young Communists
during the day I wasn't noticed but at night I zealously
tore up the flags they had forgotten to lower after their holidays,
slipping through the town with a gang of others like me.

They were fluttered in me by the same wind of hatred.
It was slavery just the same, of course, but there came a time
when I started to understand everything and weigh it.
And converting from a faith in bloody gods

to peaceful nonbelief, I celebrate Easter morning.
Though I haven't gotten used to dyeing eggs, only smashing them.

Nobody

Not all of my actions are ethical,
as befits a cultured man.

Poking someone's eye out with a stick doesn't suit
someone who wears a pocket square in his jacket
and a rose in his lapel.

Clinging to a sheep's belly while moving through a narrow opening
doesn't suit the man wearing a tuxedo,
Western culture's adept,
who likes good wine and cheese.

But nonetheless that's what happened. And it weighs the conscience?
No. Otherwise we would have been eaten,
we, who so loved ourselves,
until we were lost, took a step back,
retreated, so that our eyes could take in
a greater expanse.

And what we saw was brutality and lies
against gentleness and truth,
the troubadours' chansons (I'd like
to talk about poetry) and yet it moves.

That was, it appears, the more conscientious view,
that, apparently receding, stepping back
from the self, toward complexity. And toward hedonism?
Toward the audience of the play in which
we ourselves acted? Toward conflicts suited to dramas?
After that is it appropriate for a cultured man
to exterminate politically, measure for measure,
all those who encroached on private property?
Living once—others living just once?
Dizzyingly taking a step forward to the self,
in frenzy biting the shield,

loving one's neighbor not a stranger
in holy ecstasy?

I don't always behave ethically.
My name is Nobody too.

Another Rendezvous

She sat in the armchair as if on a throne, a woman
of unique style: piercing, somewhat tired, eyes,
a radiant face under the net of time's veil
above a long neck, breasts uncovered, sudden
and graceful movements of hands
in delicately crocheted gloves arranging things
in the deepening twilight.
And I (it's not a dream) trying to wake her,
having stopped by (she says—for a while) on my way to autumn.

Not a dream. Then what? I don't know. But I can stop
her hand half way between the glass and shadows
that enter into the arena of our undying love
which she intended to disperse with a ruler's hand...

Now I am their enemy, they try to lift me
from the ground, rocking away desires in their thawing wave—
the flame trembles, October's dusk pours through the window—
she wades against the current which has long been carrying me.
But they don't matter to me, the shadows, I care only about her
who, turning reality into a theatrical scene, strives
to encrust in it a role
which like a cliff will dissect life's turbid water.
That's why, crashed to the ground, I try to lift her into air vibrating with
        words,
into things and the will to move them to dissolving twilight,

into the impoverished, arrogant, all-comfortable luxury of doubt,
so that I would force her to forget in my arms,
so that I would move
the years, our meetings separated and filled with foreign feelings,
our own longing, congealing into sadness in our souls.

But my feet press hopelessly into the fog of these ideas
while its prop-like armchair looms so firmly on the cliff

that we pass each other again, and I have to give up,
laugh it away, hide the wrong I've suffered under a smile,

hearing how time pours out (or only this meeting's?)
as the beat of our pulses muffles in the nightfall that surrounds us.

Birdie

She rolled out of the egg that was laid
by Leda, afterwards. Black-haired, long-necked, her first
awkward movements already evidenced her coming
grace, penetrating bird eyes and lips, gently
ripening in sweetness for all who would come.

She married a lout who couldn't
satisfy his wife, that's why he scuffled later
with her lover (some say there were more than one) for nine
years "over a woman" or his offended splendor. Because of them
one member of the gang grew famous for his wanderings,
the bedding of elegant women and fidelity to his wife,
one singer went blind, later recovered his sight.
She had to lay on herself (returning through old
people's voices, the Achivi's voluptuous dreams),
adopt part of a man's role (she herself
played only women with her sudden gestures),
as imagined at that time, when in tragedies
men acted the roles of women, of course,
in her life they strived to play men,
much greater than themselves. Some succeeded,
others did not. Because the goddess
had given special privileges
only to Paris. The years passed, and her heroes
changed and aged as she fought with time.

Later, a shepherd she played with in childhood
would sometimes call her Birdie.

Palimpsests

Walking on charcoal footprints following elegant guides
(were souls burned here or something else?) I imagined the world,
later shaved their letters from my cheeks like my beard each morning,
having lathered them with the foam of my vanity.
But the letters burned in my memory as if on a wall,
dragging my pen. Filled
with thoughts not my own, perceptions, imaginings,
burdened with the past and sensations, I weave
my text, watching dejectedly
how letters change their shapes before my eyes,
how meanings merge and separate gulping
the rubbed off, shaved and washed tangle
and how apprehending consciousness adjusts to it...

And you, whose eyes shine with desire white as a snowy field,
are you also a palimpsest? Does my pen, obsessed
with aroused fluid, write into memory a new, original text,
or does it just scrape between the lines, fill lacunae and margins,
and with its foolish zeal arouse
experience like a thick tangle of roots
under the eyes' snowy field?

A Cry in Sleep

No matter what they might say or how it might appear
interesting and reasonable, a dream and that which
you are anxious to call a dream differ greatly.
You can't entangle them so easily. When you cry out
at the top of your voice in a dream, only a muffled moan
will slip out into the stuffy room. Our efforts,
my love, to try to push ourselves beyond this boundary
and there search for explanations of our feelings
are not particularly successful there: everything on this side
can be named—texts don't open the curtains,
and especially don't tell even us ourselves
why we do what we do, what we would do with our findings,
and finally, what we are searching for (you asked more than once).
Our essence, not yet overgrown with experiences? Experiences
that could be recreated, imprisoned in stringent forms
and cut out, shaved from memory, from reality?

Our hungers are from there but our actions are from this side.
Dreams giddily rock the drunken will.
What would you write on the erased board—*Vita Nuova*?
What would you do with your essence—your children?

A cry in sleep slips past its boundary greatly weakened.
Experiences collapse into the dream having nowhere else.

Spring in the Middle of Fall

My thoughts grow heavy, curl back into the ground
bursting before like blossoms and ripening fruits.
Suddenly on the windowsill a tiny bird,
not having managed to fly off to oblivion,
ticks with its claws on the tin parchment
and the soul grows confused.

And the soul blossoms in the fall, but not like
late dahlias, gladioli or asters,
and not like chrysanthemums
but like an insane plum-tree. I shave letters,
write new, unexpected symbols.

Mansion residents look over my shoulder with derision—
there is little here to be believed. But the front
of spring is wide as it is in April—ice fortresses collapse,
the marble of statues chaps and crumbles,
from ever closer gallops bad news.

Mansion residents soberly drink whiskey.
Spring—they say—in the middle of fall?
Interesting, yes, yes, on the way to winter.

A Shabby Dwelling

The air is thicker here, fragrances
loom like a former forest of conceptions.

Though I could always find her scent
through the deluding perfumes of ideas
with love's perfect sense of smell.

Always grasped by the tightly-stretched reins,
barely across the span away from desired things,
always restrained at the last minute.
She said she liked to walk on the edges of knives,
trying not to collapse into my (oh if only into my!) passion
which had no bottom, no boundaries, no response.

Once in my line of sight her naked body glittered
like waxed marble. I began to turn...
Not into prey, no, but a tool, just as earlier
I had been transformed into the tool of my desire—with no
other hungers, thoughts, identities, realities—
animal on the rein.

I felt completely normal then, led down the street
by another woman. I could smell her from a distance,
as always, surrounded by a fence that did not contain her fragrance.

Her graceful quick steps rang in my blood.
I don't remember what happened next. When we had
almost passed by one another, I jumped onto her
wanting to embrace her with my front legs, and yelping
she staggered under my body's weight, the guide mumbled
that I had never done that before. I was wearing a muzzle.
She didn't recognize me. Our eyes did not meet.
Our eyes did not meet.

Didn't recognize me? Let her try
to remember. For if I wasn't the only one
like that under the reins... let her try. Circe.

The body is a shabby dwelling
and even desire is more stable.

A Discussion About Lions

She said she saw on television how a lioness
is impregnated: she is first pollinated by one, then by
his brother, and later by a stray. No emotions were involved.
Probably because—as the narrator commented—
lionesses rarely conceive on the first try.

I answered that once Atalanta (*fugiens*),
nursed on bear's milk, unsurpassable,
promised to marry the one who could outrun her,
and she killed the ones who lost.

Then someone named Melanion or Hippomenes, who had
three golden apples from the Hesperidian gardens, ran
and threw them one by one just when she caught up
and he reached the finish line alive. (I don't know,
perhaps it was gentleness and love, hands
on your desired body.) And they got married
and instantly made passionate love, and once
they did that in Zeus' temple, and the angered
god turned them into lions (Zeus and the Greeks for some reason
believed that only leopards could impregnate lions),
that is to say—they would live in chastity.

The apples were stolen, and god, as always,
lacked an understanding of nature. So let them be lions.
It's only a form,
one of many.

The Goddess of Oblivion

It's a woman, hanging laundry
on a rope, flapping in the wind, damp,
for a moment stuck with what is no longer there.

Ugly, angular, unattractive

our mother
of oblivion.

Outlines

1.
I can name everything,
can outline everything.

2.
Even your oval belly I encircle
with the oval of a poem, "my dear."

3.
Language from Culture, which belongs to us,
which we created, carefully tended, whose pinnacle

4.
we darkened with the clouds of secret rituals,
and we forbade them to witness

5.
for those whose creative powers arise on their own from nothing,
whose swollen ovals encompass, even give birth to us...

6.
It is hardest to perceive that. How we are born—
with Culture or without?

7.
If without, then everything is determined by initiations,
which we fulfill in secret and without hardship.

8.
But each of us has experienced
how little they change.
That's why doubt remains.

9.
And what if with? Could Culture
conceal itself in these strange creations?

10.
Then we enclose the mother and child in the oval
and solemnly announce the doctrine of the second birth.

11.
Yes, we tamed nature, fettered your strengths,
with rituals bound the demigods
who laid you—
we know it, don't lie.

12.
We transformed them into wooden idols, and now
with our magical dances don't let them come to life again,

13.
because we know, on full moon nights you still dream
of their long fecund organs and hands that grasp your backs.

14.
That's why we can't calm down,
that's why the worm of suspicion, like self-
deception, gnaws at your brain.

15.
That's why we rape, murder, display power and·rule,
until we believe that this all is natural—
so much death everywhere that it cannot be multiplied.

16.
She has outlined everything in a tight oval
which it is better not to see, because our rituals don't function.

17.
My dear, to protect myself
from choosing your freedom from your governance of me,

18.
from fear, from doubting myself, from your
inclination to surrender to demigods in my imagination,
I surround your image with an oval as if on an old postcard,

19.
I meditate, incense the gods, burn
my heart's desires like the sun burns the desert,

20.
I break the attachments
and stuff myself with tranquility...

21.
But the worm gnaws through it.

22.
I cast off norms, truths, regulations, go out of my mind,
my will, guilts and beliefs, find delight only in semblances,

23.
reel in ecstasies or shudder in catharses
until the worm suddenly stirs and calls me.

24.
Finally, numb with horror, I see
how desire outlines me within you like a womb.

New Guinea, The Abelam Forest

About Starlings After Yet Another Five Years

I live now like a starling
in a small computer box,
cast my songs into the world net
far, wide, though fewer ears probably
hear them than yours, my brother,
which you warble on the roof fluttering
your wings home again after winter,
transformed into a beckoning voice.

That's not how it works for me, and even
the changing seasons don't stir my feelings,
as if I had left their circle and had ended up
on a straightaway, at whose end
is the small strip that separates realities...

The way myth pretending to be history
confuses reason and truth,
broken time turning into a straight line,
and so my poetic identity
tempts the virtual bird
to jug all year (out of habit?)
on a branch gilded by intoxication.

Portrait

The paint cracked
like Leonardo's, Vermeer's
like Rembrandt's.
Time is our disease. Unfulfillments.
And if—I say—some small patch falls off
who will know how to return it to a forgetful past?
Will restorers reconstruct color,
variable semitones?
And if they do, won't time
change them at a different rate?

Passions are our disease. Unsatisfied.
Fissuring the coating,
transforming us into puzzles
in the banality of mirrors...

And if—I say—in that patch is a former
reflection of your soul or the shadow of a lover's face?

Turning back you'd say you saw
how quickly you disappeared into the crowd,
as if you had dissolved in paint.

The Faceless

No, if that's believing I won't confess to it.
I need knowledge, need a guide—
the land of the dead is full of error,
it is thick with souls, likenesses.
I don't remember her face.
But some succubus can pretend to be her,
easily adapt a mask.
You at least had seen her, your Euridice, you knew
how she looked, why are you descending there, arrows
of your hymns had a purpose. But I did not.
I suspect that it's my soul's
face, which mirrors don't reflect,
which can be seen only on the surface of Lethe,
on the other shore, emptied of words.
Each succubus is able to pretend
to be her, the way women do here, in illusion,
without a sense of foreboding,
intently watching my movements, my lies.
They hate the faceless woman but want to be her.
And I for a moment want to be deceived,
become acquainted, almost trust...
It's not enough for me to know she's in the land
of the dead, if I believed in you, or elsewhere.
I'd want to see her, rest calmly in her arms,
even if for eternity.

I'm not speaking to explain anything here.

Autumn's Flowers

Dahlias, gladioli and asters,
blossoms lifted with dignity to the cooling air,
and your multicolored cap,
with all their hues
radiant above the garden.
You say: this autumn
stole my hair
and scattered it in spider webs
on stalks of dry grass,
on passionate memories,
on brightening waters.
Men are finishing picking
the small garden's harvest,
the barrow squeaks with cranes.
—It's hardest to endure uncertainty—
you say with dignity to air filled with sunshine.
A cold wind blows through
the dahlias, gladioli, and asters.

The Square

Desolate is the roof where the cat sat...
Ezra Pound, Canto 39.

An empty square, where the monument stood,
there's no pedestal, pissed on by dogs,
wind brings a scrap of thin plastic,
it unexpectedly jumps into the monument's place
and once again settles down beyond it. The subconscious
sucks up reality—I tell my young companion
now no one will be able to explain
what, how, and why it changed.
What, how, and why it lives
in someone's memory—as time passes,
it looks more and more like a graveyard.

Vita Nuova

Morning's hinges creak, waking me,
Titans moor on the ocean's bottom,
and Phoebus rolls out of the cave of ideas
in a glittering chariot
as if in a new Ferrari through the factory gates
into a fresh world revised by the morning papers...

And the oblivions of the abyss swallow night's dreams
together with those who lifted their heads
before our gods, paying no attention
to financial markets, economic indexes,
commodity prices, currency exchange rates.
The battle is won—Gaia's sons
are cast by the gods to Tartarus.
A new life explodes in images.

Phoebus' steeds never dreamed of such speed.

A Troubled Year

That year the heavens sent many omens
promising disastrous events,
which our decaying morality demanded,
but the year ended
according to all the calendars
and nothing happened.

Except that the supreme interpreter
of omens died.

Also Died

to Gerardo, for reasons of literary scholarship

The water in the pond died of longing
having waited in vain for an intent gaze.

Love died in that water
as bodies entwined.

The poet died on the shore
having stopped admiring himself.

The light in the eyes died, the deep of the pupils
gone opaque, having found no reflection.

Billions of gray cells dying carried our words
to the other side of the mirror's glass.

The hard disk was broken
by the virus of self perception.

Wanting to Be

       you must be like everyone else—
at least a catholic
at least a moral christian (*depends on the place*)
at least a jew
at least a muslim
at least a promethean
       you must love your neighbor as yourself
       and yourself—endlessly (*like a Christian*)
       and unlove a stranger
       if resources are not sufficient
       you must say: *and how will I now and how will I now*
       and how will I now die and where will I go? and then
       you will have to answer immediately: *I*
       will rise from the grave with a body spackled with impurities
       and will be brought to the last judgment—
       if you want to be like everyone else don't try
       to avoid juridical procedures
       (*though they too depend on the place*)—
       so will be brought to trial flipping the finger in his pocket
       ha, I got my body back so screw you
at least a circus man (*these stunts*)
at least a social activist (*others?*)
at least a native (*kalashnikovs and whiskey*)
at least a roundworm in its place (*good feeding*)
       you must love yourself passionately and gently
at least a representative of an opposing fratria
at least as I said a promethean
       (*a wife for one people's gratitude for the other*)
       you must love yourself—*l o v e*
       and if I have already rebelled against god
       or the gods then with full stature like the titans
       with full stature which is not at all low
at least a child of nature (*a prize*)
at least (*hangovers*) a club hopper
at least a frequent lover (*a discount coupon*)
at least (*coffee*) a buyer of the morning paper

and its reader (*pridefully*)
at least a television watcher (*chopped off heads*)
at least a radio listener (*speaking*)
at least (*laurels for*) an award-winning poet
at least him who seeks a career (*the grace of heaven*)
       and struggles with the angel on the stairs
       or otherwise reads the bible (*amen*)
at least one who goes to church on Sundays
at least a buddhist (*zen*) or krishna (*hare*)
at least (*steering wheel*) one who can't manage without a car
at least one who doesn't believe in god (*catechismvsa*)
       and similar foolishness (*prasty szadei*)
       we require loving oneself
       does that require resourcefulness? no
       but we need it to suggest to others
       the successes we've had, being loved
       or at least deserving of envy, or else
       respected out of fear (*just in case*)
at least achilles without heels
at least a heel to the teeth (*to another*)
at least Nothing
       you must *l o v e* yourself
       wanting to be

I Met that Starling Later in Dublin

He tiptoed warbling in the November
airport, just past the arrivals door,
on occasion trundling to escape
approaching shoes, sometimes
turning his beak towards something,
but holding it back at the last minute,
understanding the target wasn't something to eat.

I have nothing to add about myself.
I had wandered in there for just a moment.

Confrontation in the Museum

Dickheaded Cypress,
(I am addressing the god hiding in us,
controlling our hands and minds,
or perhaps them both—Apollo and Dionysus), how long
is the way from your coarse amulet,
with the body crucified by two genders
conjuring a blunt world,
to this marble maiden with firm breasts
and youth's back, Hellene,
reviving the body in the fire of our glance
betraying the master who strode long ago
on the golden rooftop in moonlight and still
how long the time to our
barbaric conceptualizing,
in single-use forms suppressing
unnecessary small ideas
like private sexual organs
controlling our hands and minds.

Cave Phenomena

They say carbonic acid melts soft rocks,
they flow away on underground rivers, drip from stalactites,
grow stalagmites, in coves
jam together as small coffins like junks,
seen from an airplane,
and in those small coffins—just lift the lid—
you'll see your days,
the shapes of your thoughts, as if cerements
of somewhat whiter fog, a thin membrane
lying on former illusions.

And in the mouths of rivers!
How nobly they would float out to sea,
would meet the first wave...

And my loves sleep there with eyes closed,
with smiles barely visible in the corners of their mouths,
reflecting in shimmering surfaces...

And my verses sleep
in the printer's paint cases....

Time's acids ate away the soft rocks
from the monolith of consciousness—
the caves weave, branch like a labyrinth
in a once firm mass,
melted rocks drip
in tears from your eyes, roll down your cheeks, leaving
funeral membranes and empty spaces
to lay down the world
in the hour of death,
to begin a new life,
arrange decorations and raise
the curtain of the new performance,
or equip offices and begin to expand commerce,

or see the house, the grove,
highway or brook collapse.

And then swing away in rivers toward the mouths
slowly, somewhat ceremoniously or even pompously—
in each coffin a poem or a medal,
or some other small fetish—
thinking: if only we don't tip over
in the first wave.

The Transfigured Stairs

There were only three stairs to the porch
but they suddenly began to shine differently,
as if in a new light that holds things,
torn from memory in old photographs,
and the house remained in another time,
became unreachable,
and my "I" cracked, liquified.
Lord, you won't be able to put a foot on it,
won't walk across the image fixer's lake, won't step
into the soul's house on the other side
whose window shutters
are banged so hard by the heavens' winds.

Haiku, Senryu, and Other Very Short Poems

And out of the past
wind carries blossom petals
that blanket the stream.

*

Blossoms drift away
on the river. This nonsense
is ending once more!

*

The blackbird's song placed
a period on the text
of insomnia.

*

The furies' bright eyes
found both of us in the dark
of the far mountains.

*

Your book has many
things, but the dividing mark
here is simply you.

*

Down along your cheek
red as a maple I roll
in an angry tear.

*

From the foam of dream
emerging into semblance
we smile so shyly.

*

The flood of words has
ended. Autumn's full moon is
void as an echo.

*

With fingernails of
leaves I hold fast to the tree
outside the window.

*

The world that flourished
and shrank just recently is
expanding again.

*

Water carries time
with the dust from a soiled rag
away down the sink.

*

The dog of the house
reads the smells of the forest
in instinct's volume.

*

Warm January.
The ground is soft and slimy.
I don't want to die.

*

Bottle of whiskey,
I'm empty already too
but not yet lucid.

*

Lakes beneath the ice,
it's time to chop holes in it—
all the world is one.

*

The sun's small rabbit
hops along the back of chairs
into the autumn.

*

In winter's sick room
the finch is finishing to
recover from it.

*

flow of wind
flow of senses
flood of yellow

*

Petals of tulips.
Angels—the lone emptiness
of our consciousness.

*

Gray rain
on a leaden sea.
I return to you.

*

They migrate in zeroes
and ones in autumn
like my poetry.

*

Far from the earth
but not closer to heaven.
Valleys drown in blossoms.

*

The world is empty.
So I fill you again with
meaning, mountain ash.

*

The river carries our
two faces under the bridge.
One more October.

*

Cicadas chirp.
The telephone doesn't work.
Edo.

*

Fields of rice.
In one of them sprouted
beds of gravestones.

*

The stairs of temples
are much steeper in August.
Carp at the surface.

*

And for twenty yen
you can enter into
the Buddha's belly.

*

Cicadas droning.
Me with *The Lonely Planet*
in my backpack.

*

Small fish
in Lake Ohrid,
great poets
on the bridge in Struga.

*

The current—
"day and night, summer and winter"
complains the river fish.

*

A white butterfly
against the fence staves—
a violin melody.

*

Lithuanian fish
fingering syllables
in an autumn lake.

*

The knife of morning
slices through the powdered crust,
the sun slips away.

*

The passing freight train
rattles on the truck's windows
the dry season's rain.

*

She stands at the top
of the stairs, young, short-skirted.
My mother lies dead.

*

Plant trees in Edo
and the cicadas will chirp
when their time comes.

*

The sparrow chases
a fly for her nested brood,
in the church—High Mass.

*

The cat has been pitched
to the pond after a frog
by her own instinct.

*

The rains of summer.
Both of us home with the cat,
a snail at home too.

*

The wood is piled up,
the road for the Sun to climb
to the skies is paved.

The Carp

It's as cramped here as a supermarket—on both sides of the glass
two crowds of the condemned rub their flanks.
She stabbed with her finger and said: I want that one.
The saleswoman began to mix
the aquarium's suffocating water with a ladle.

I tried to twist away, that's why the fishing took so long,
but the finger's stinger already stuck into my heart.

I thrashed in the oxygen's abundance and gasped
pulled out into unfamiliar air
thinned by my own desires.

Then the saleswoman stuck me
into a plastic bag—this world's
invisible but sealed border pressed tight.

For a moment I still imagined how her graceful fingers
would separate my bones from soft braised flesh,
how I will let myself go across those dreamed lips
into the hungry grave in her belly.

The Ebony Tower
(Scenario for a short film)

An autumn landscape, morning fog,
a telephone booth on thin wire legs
gets out of sequence, a voice:
hello, I can't describe the world
in terms of my own shadow,
do you hear that, bitch? Give that apple back,
your embers have died inside me, don't rekindle
the wasting fire's reflections.

The telephone booth
slinks out of use.

Fragmentation: Phrygians
(*Scenario for a video installation*)

Quickly—he shouts—quickly dismantle the monitor,
everyone his part—and into those red bags,
boarding has already begun!
We disconnect smoothly in small sections
and with little bags—to the security control.
Everyone passes, sit on chairs like in garden beds.
Flying into place, easily (quickly, quickly)
we connect the parts again, the operator
pushes the button, but instead of this
well-acted video installation
on the fragmented screen, our heads
sprout wearing red bags
as if Phrygian caps... What's this all about—
the director howls—reload,
take my memory! But turning it on again—
it's the same result—exhausted by commands Phrygian heads,
which are replaced every five minutes
by a charming commercial across the screen
about some sort of winged creatures
and it incites a timid hope that everything will be all right
and eventually the scene we long for will appear...
But no—it's those Phrygians again.
                    The audience
has already poured out into the hall. It's a goddess—a small group
of girls quacks pointing fingers. Then the director
puts his finger to his temple
and shoots himself down.

The Difficulties of Integrating into Society

(Scenario for a computer game)

Snowflakes fall lazily,
a dog barks,
its voice sticks the snowflakes into lumps,
snow bombs fall from heaven,
a mouse helps the dog,
it has nine lives
which flow away as a song plays:
> I just wanted to say
> I just wanted to say
> That I live in this yard.

Bump. Want to begin again?

Notes

p. 61 *St. Elizabeth's Hospital.* Parts of a poetry fusion made by Craig Czury from the works of patients at St. E's Hospital are used in this text.

p. 97 In *Wanting to Be*, the book title *Catechismvsa Prasti Szadei* (Simple Words of the Catechism) by Martynas Mažvydas. (The Old Lithuanian Catechism, 1547) refers to the first book published in Lithuanian.

About the Translator

Jonas Zdanys is the author of forty-three other books, thirty-nine of them collections of his own poetry, written in English and in Lithuanian, and of his translations of Lithuanian poetry and prose into English. He has received a number of prizes and book awards for his own poetry and for his translations. He held administrative and faculty positions at Yale University from 1980 to 1998, where he began and taught the poetry translation workshop, and served as the State of Connecticut's Chief Academic Officer and Associate Commissioner of Higher Education from 1998 to 2009. He serves currently as Professor of English at Sacred Heart University, where he teaches creative writing and seminars on modern poetry.

www.ingramcontent.com/pod-product-compliance
Lightning Source LLC
Chambersburg PA
CBHW020944090426
42736CB00010B/1251